Thoughtful Quotes

For Your Notes

Anna J. Campbell

Dedication

~ For my husband, Brean Campbell

Thank you for always encouraging me to keep dreaming, to keep reaching, and to keep achieving! You have inspired me to think outside of the box, dig really deep and to know that I am truly never alone. Love you!

Photo courtesy of Joel Dunn.

Thoughtful Quotes For You Notes

Introduction

When my daughter was little, I remember the pure joy she had every day when it was time to check the mail. She had such anticipation of going with her daddy to see what new creations would be waiting for her.

Her loving grandparents would often send cards and fun gifts. Even though she didn't receive something wonderful every day, the excitement and joy kept her looking forward to the afternoon trip to the mailbox.

My passion for writing letters stemmed from letters my sister Jenny would send me throughout our teenage years as we grew up 335 miles apart. She would share her adventures, dreams, and short stories while I shared my ideas and experiences with her.

My mother then continued the letter-writing joy with me as she sent me encouragement and advice when I left home. After getting married, my mother-in-law Lisa Campbell joined my letter writing crusade by sending inspirational cards for every occasion! These women are why my daughter became infatuated with the process of sending drawings and stories through the mail. As adults, we have often lost that excitement as fun cards turn into bills and jury duty summons.

The joy of receiving a thoughtful note from someone who took the time to pick out a card, write a little message and drop it in the mail is priceless.

Spreading love is easy and fun when you have beautiful cards and loving words available at your fingertips!

I have gathered a selection of my favorite quotes, poems, and rhymes appropriate for a wide selection of occasions and reasons.

It is customary to send cards for many occasions throughout the year, including sympathy, birthdays, anniversaries, graduations, weddings, and sweet new babies.

May you find many opportunities to send sweet cards.

~ Anna Campbell

Photo courtesy of Carolyn V.

Contents

Photo courtesy of Sara Cottle.

Acknowledgments

My life is filled with memories of amazing people who have come and gone. Each person has left an imprint on my mind, heart, and soul.

I would especially like to thank my dear friend Elizabeth Fogt (Fogt rhymes with Note) for giving me the inspiration to follow my dreams and enjoy every moment of my life.

My life wouldn't be full without my husband Brean, daughter Jay, parents Jere & Joan Wilson, and all of my extended family and friends.

Thank you for inspiring me.

Thoughtful Quotes For You Notes

Photo courtesy of Kirsty TG.

Chapter 1

Inspirational Quotes

I find myself using this chapter the most as I write a love note to a dear friend or just a quick thank you note to a fellow club member.

Knowing that someone else appreciates us and the things we do helps shine a light on a service that may often be taken for granted.

Take a moment today and think about someone who has done something kind for you or someone you know. Write them a quick thank you and drop it in the mail.

You will inspire more people than you may ever know.

~ Anna

Anna J. Campbell

Photo courtesy of Freddy Castro

mineratl.com

"Today, I realized that anything is possible, and the only person standing in my way was myself! We can do anything we put our minds to, and I believe in you!"
Anna J. Campbell

"Champions are propelled by Desire, Not compelled by Fear."
Author Unknown

"Good morning beautiful! Yesterday is over. All your slip-ups are forgiven. The score is zero. Make it positive Today!"
Author Unknown

"The biggest communication problem is we do not listen to understand. We listen to reply."
Author Unknown

"We make a living by what we get; we make a life by what we give."
Winston Churchill (1874 – 1965)

"Never regret anything that has happened in your life, it cannot be changed, undone or forgotten. So take it as a lesson learned and move on."
Author Unknown

Anna J. Campbell

Photo courtesy of Alessandra Espinoza.

"Art is one of the most intimate ways to learn about yourself and the world around you."
 Anna Campbell

"Life is not about waiting for the storm to pass, it's about learning to Dance in the Rain."
Author Unknown

"I am not what has happened to me. I am what I choose to become."
Carl Jung (1875 – 1961)

"The Secret to having it all... is Believing you already do..."
Author Unknown

"Stop worrying about what you have to lose and start focusing on what you have to gain."
Author Unknown

"If you are always racing to the next moment what happens to the one you're in?"
Author Unknown

"Some people come into your life as blessings, others come into your life as lessons."
Author Unknown

"Life is so much brighter when we focus on what truly matters..."
Author Unknown

Photo courtesy of Wijdan Mq.

"Judging a person does not define who they are. It defines who you are."
Author Unknown

"Life is a like a mirror: It'll smile at you if you smile at it."
Author Unknown

"Attitude is a little thing that makes a big difference."
Winston Churchill (1875 – 1965)

"It is the mark of an educated mind to be able to entertain a thought without accepting it."
Aristotle (384 BC – 322 BC)

"I will take waiting over settling any day this week."
Author Unknown

"No one is perfect that's why pencils have erasers."
Author Unknown

"I am not afraid of storms, for I am learning how to sail my ship."
Louisa May Alcott (1832 – 1888)

"Worry is a thief that robs us of our confidence and asks us why. When we should be asking, Why not!"
Anna J. Campbell

Photo courtesy of Giulia Bertelli.

unpeusauvage.com

"Every day is a new beginning, stay away from what might have been and look towards what can be."
Author Unknown

"You are amazing and don't you forget it!"
Author Unknown

"Never give up on anybody. Miracles happen every day."
Author Unknown

"Stop acting so small, you are the universe in ecstatic motion."
Rumi (1207 – 1273)

"If you wait for perfect conditions, you'll never get anything done."
Author Unknown

"Dancing is silent poetry."
Simonides (556 BC – 468 BC)

"We tend to forget that happiness doesn't come as a result of getting something we don't have, but rather of recognizing and appreciating what we do have."
Frederick Keonig (1774 -1833)

"There is only one way to happiness and that is to cease worrying about things which are beyond the power of our will."
Epictetus (55 – 135)

Photo courtesy of Rebecca

rebeccaleecreative.com

"Each day is a new opportunity. Stand up, walk into the light, and shine!"
Anna J. Campbell

"You deserve a day where worries don't get in the way of anything. A day where even if some people are insensitive or unkind, you're not going to mind because the blessings in your life are far greater than the burdens that people are trying to place on you. ~ Stay positive!"
Author Unknown

"A smile is the prettiest thing you can wear."
Author Unknown

"Educating the mind without educating the heart is like no education at all."
Aristotle (384 BC – 322 BC)

"May you always find new roads to travel;
New horizons to explore;
New dreams to call your own."
Author Unknown

"Embracing life can be amazing. Each day is another opportunity to meet another friend along our journey."
Anna J. Campbell

"Every child is gifted. They just unwrap their packages at different times."
Author Unknown

Photo courtesy of My Life Journal.

mylifejournal.co

"We are the music makers and we are the dreamer of dreams."
Arthur O'Shaughnessy (1844 – 1881)

"When the milk is splattered all over the floor and those little eyes are looking at you for your reaction, remember what really matters.

It takes 5 minutes to clean up spilled milk; it takes much longer to clean up a broken spirit."
Rebecca Eames (1641 – 1721)

"You can often change your circumstances by changing your attitude."
Eleanor Roosevelt (1884 – 1962)

"He who has a 'why' to live, can bear with almost any 'how'."
Friedrich Nietzsche (1844 – 1900)

"The true measure of a man is how he treats someone who can do him absolutely no good."
Samuel Johnson (1709 – 1784)

"Perfection is achieved, not when there is nothing more to add, but when there is nothing left to take away."
Antoine de Saint Exupery (1900 – 1940)

"Obstacles are those frightful things you see when you take your eyes off your goal."
Henry Ford (1863 – 1947)

Photo courtesy of Iva Lopes.

instagram.com/create.for.yourself

"Success usually comes to those who are too busy to be looking for it."
Henry David Thoreau (1817 – 1862)

"Raise your words, not voice. It is rain that grows flowers, not thunder."
Rumi (1207 – 1273)

"The future belongs to those who believe in the beauty of their dreams."
Eleanor Roosevelt (1884 – 1962)

"Good morning! You are love, life, and hope. How will you use this gift of a brand new day?"
Anna J. Campbell

"There comes a point in your life when you realize who really matters, who never did, and who always will."
Author Unknown

"When I let go of what I am, I become what I might me."
Lao Tzu (531 BC)

"Only those who will risk going too far, can possibly find out how far one can go."
T. S. Eliot (1888 – 1965)

Photo courtesy of Mitchell Luo.

Chapter 2

Thankful Quotes

I am always on the hunt for fun and loving quotes to use in my Thank You notes. These have served me well in a wide range of ways, from business to pleasure.

When picking out a quote, I try to connect how I would like the person to feel when they read my card. In this way, each quote you use will have a maximum effect!

If you have a large number of thank you cards for sending out, try breaking them down into groups of 5 or 10. This way, you will have enough energy to share with your recipients as you write each note.

~ Anna

Photo courtesy of Emily Park.

"It is not Happy people who are Thankful; it is Thankful people who are Happy."
Unknown Author

"Let today be the start of something new."
Author Unknown

"It is the sweet simple things in life
Which are the real ones after all."
Laura Ingalls Wilder (1867 – 1957)

"I cried because I had no shoes
Until I met a man with no feet."
Persian Proverb

"Appreciation can make a day, even change a life.
Your willingness to put it into words is all that is necessary."
Margaret Cousins (1878 – 1954)

"Most of the shadows in this life
are caused by our standing
in our own sunshine."
Ralph Waldo Emerson (1803 – 1882)

"A thankful heart is a happy heart."
Author Unknown

"We did not inherit the Earth from our ancestors; we borrow it from our children."
Author Unknown

Photo courtesy of Annie Spratt.

anniespratt.com

"Each day I am thankful for
Nights that turned into mornings
Friends that turned into family
Dreams that turned into reality
And likes that turned into love."
Unknown Author

"Give without remembering. Take without
forgetting."
Elizabeth Bibesco (1897 – 1945)

"Life is a gift, I accept it.
Life is an adventure, I dare it.
Life is a mystery, I'm unfolding it.
Life is a puzzle, I'm solving it.
Life is a game, I play it.
Life can be a struggle, I'm facing it.
Life is beauty, I praise it.
Life is an opportunity, I took it.
Life is my mission, I'm fulfilling it."
Author Unknown

"I am thankful for the lessons I have learned and
the friends who are by my side. Love is my
greatest healer."
Anna J. Campbell

"I'm thankful for so many things, but mostly, God.
Without him I'd have nothing else to be thankful
for."
Author Unknown

Photo courtesy of Phuong Minh Luu.

"Be kind
Be thoughtful
Be genuine
But most of all
Be thankful."
Author Unknown

"Thanks for being the friend who always believed in me, who always understood; who always accepted me and always cared."
Author Unknown

"Today I am thankful for my past which lead me to this moment where my dream journey begins anew..."
Author Unknown

"May your day be filled with love, kindness, gratitude and a little bit of chocolate."
Author Unknown

"Let us be grateful to people who make us happy; they are the charming gardeners who make our souls blossom."
Author Unknown

Photo courtesy of Kevin Butz.

Chapter 3

Sympathy Quotes

These are the saddest cards I must write and are often not read for some time after being received. Losing a dear loved one affects our day to day lives.

Sometimes a kind and a brief note will help to lighten the heavy load.

~ Anna

Photo courtesy of Sarah Evans.

designbundles.net/illuztrate

"Tenderly may time heal your sorrow
Gently may friends ease your pain
Softly may peace replace heartaches, and may
warmest memories remain."
Author Unknown

"May the constant love of caring friends soften
your sadness.
May cherished memories bring you moments of
comfort.
May lasting peace surround your grieving heart."
Author Unknown

"A sad thing in life is that sometimes you meet
someone who means a lot to you only to find out
in the end that it was never bound to be and you
just have to let go."
Author Unknown

"Death leaves a heartache no one can heal, love
leaves a memory no one can steal."
Author Unknown

Photo courtesy of Jere Wilson.

Chapter 4

Compassionate Quotes

There are when our friends need a little pick me up. And a sweet note will be the perfect remedy.

I often try and include words or images that bring a smile to my face to bring some sunshine to the recipient's day too!

Humor has also been a good remedy for when a friend is blue after a temporary setback. Words of reassurance have been useful for a severe setback, such as losing a job or a critical opportunity.

~ Anna

Photo courtesy of Sippakorn Yamkasikorn.

shutterstock.com/g/sippakornyam

"Always laugh when you can. It is cheap medicine."
Lord Byron (1788 – 1824)

"Welcome to this glorious new day! Today, as we face our challenges, remember that the moments will pass, and we will thrive. Together, we can get through anything. "
Anna J. Campbell

"How does one become a Butterfly? You must want to fly so much that you are willing to give up being a caterpillar."
Author Unknown

"The joy we see must come from within. We must be building the life we dream of, not expecting others to provide it for us. When we are our strongest, we can make the most daring, courageous, and miraculous decisions of our lives. You are an inspiration to everyone around you."
Anna J. Campbell

"Don't allow your wounds to turn you into a person you are not."
Author Unknown

"Challenges are for the mighty, are you ready?"
Anna J. Campbell

Photo courtesy of Annie Spratt.

anniespratt.com

Never regret the decisions you have made throughout your life; they cannot be changed, undone, or forgotten. So take them as a lesson learned and move on."
Anna J. Campbell

"You are beautiful. You are strong. I love you just the way you are."
Anna J. Campbell

Photo courtesy of Carolyn V.

Chapter 5

Quotes of Love

There are moments in our lives where passion and romance create opportunities for us to share words that bring our hearts closer together or provide an encouraging word that love will still exist.

May we recognize these moments and take a few moments to share words of inspiration with others.

~ Anna

Photo courtesy of Elena Mozhvilo.

instagram.com/miracledaystudio

"Every once in a while, in the middle of an ordinary life, *Love* gives us a *fairytale*."
Author Unknown

"There is always somebody that loves you. Always."
Author Unknown

"For it was not into my ear you whispered, but into my Heart. It was not my lips you kissed, but my Soul."
American singer, actress and vaudevillian
Judy Garland (born Frances Ethel Gumm 1922 - 1969)

"Because of you, I believe all things are possible."
Anna J. Campbell

"True love isn't easy, but it must be fought for. Because once you find it, it can never be replaced."
Author Unknown

"And then my soul saw you and it kind of went 'Oh there you are. I've been looking for you.'"
Author Unknown

"Be with a man who ruins your lipstick, not your mascara."
Author Unknown

"I like 'me' a little bit more when I'm with you."
Author Unknown

Photo courtesy of Nick Fewings.

instagram.com/jannerboy62

"And we will sit upon the rocks,
And see the shepherds feed their flocks
By shallow rivers, to whose falls
Melodious birds sing madrigals.

And I will make thee beds of roses
And a thousand fragrant posies;
A cap of flowers, and a kirtle
Embroider'd all with leaves of myrtle.

A gown made of the finest wool
Which from our pretty lambs we pull;
Fair-lined slippers for the cold,
With buckles of the purest gold."
The Passionate Shepherd to His Love by English
playwright, poet, and translator of the
Elizabethan era
Christopher Marlowe (1564 – 1593)

"I am thankful for the lessons I have learned and
the friends who are by my side. Love is my
greatest healer."
Anna J. Campbell

"Do everything with so much love in your heart
that you would never want to do it any other
way."
Author Unknown

"I just want… to thank you for being my reason
to look forward to the next day."
Author Unknown

Photo courtesy of Marina Grynykha.

grynykha.com

"Thank you… for staying event if you had every reason to leave. Thank you for making it easier when life gets hard."
Author Unknown

"Woke up this morning, and all is right in my world. Love, peace, and joy are all around us. Embrace and care for each other."
Anna J. Campbell

"I love you for giving your heart o me
and trusting me with your pride.
I love you for wanting me
and needing me by your side.

I love you for the emotions
I never knew I had.
I love you for making me smile
whenever I feel sad.

I love you for your thoughts of me
where I'm always on your mind.
I love you for finding that part of me
that I never thought I'd find.
I love you for the way you are
and for how you make me feel.
But most of all I LOVE YOU
'cuz I know you're mine for real."
Author Unknown

"Your love is like a waterfall. It carries me away each time."
Anna J. Campbell

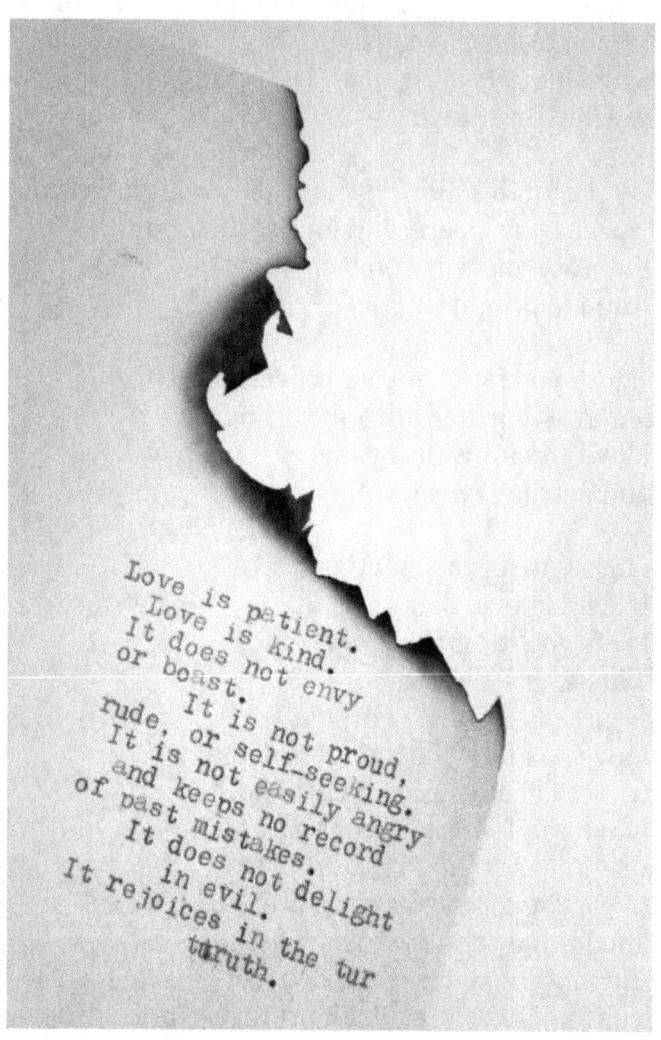

Love is patient.
Love is kind.
It does not envy
or boast.
It is not proud,
rude, or self-seeking.
It is not easily angry
and keeps no record
of past mistakes.
It does not delight
in evil.
It rejoices in the tur
thruth.

Photo courtesy of Leighann Blackwood.

ohleighann.com

"I never thought anyone would ever make me smile, laugh, and capture my heart as fast as you have."
Author Unknown

Anna J. Campbell

Photo courtesy of Jere Wilson.

Chapter 6

Humorous Quotes

When our loved ones are feeling blue, humorous quotes bring a ray of sunshine into their day. Sometimes a simple word can change their entire day!

Sometimes, receiving a joke in the mail can keep us laughing and feeling loved because someone cared enough to jot down a few words and drop it in the mail.

You have the power to transform an ordinary day into a moment of pure joy!

~ Anna

Photo courtesy of Aidas Ciziunas.

"Don't get confused between my
Personality and my Attitude.
My Personality is who I am,
My Attitude depends on who you are."
Author Unknown

"The tallest oak in the forest was once just a little
nut that held its ground."
Author Unknown

"If you can't get rid of the skeleton in your closet,
you'd best teach it to dance."
George Bernard Shaw (1856 – 1950)

"The difference between 'involvement' and
'commitment' is like an eggs-and-ham breakfast:
the chicken was 'involved' - the pig was
'committed'."
Author Unknown

"Some cause happiness wherever they go;
others, whenever they go."
Oscar Wilde (1854 – (1900)

Photo Courtesy of Linda Segerfeldt.

Chapter 7

Quotes for Family & Friends

I love sending notes to my family and friends at random times throughout the years, but I don't always know what to say. These fun quotes have served me well for many different occasions.

Receiving cards in the mail for no real reason makes the note all the more special. Because just knowing that the person was top of mind for you brings a sense of love and belonging.

~ Anna

Photo courtesy of Alice Pasqual.

"Sometimes it is impossible to know where you
are headed without reflecting on where you
came from. Understanding your heritage, your
roots and your ancestry is an important part of
carving out your future."
Author Unknown

"Step Mom,
You entered our family at my father's side
With wisdom and patience.
Though of your flesh I was not conceived,
You cared and filled an empty need."
Author Unknown

"A step parent is so much more than just a
parent;
They made the choice to love when they didn't
have to."
Author Unknown

"Family ~ Like branches on a tree we all grow in
different directions yet our roots remain as one."
Author Unknown

"Having a place to go is home
Having someone to love is family
Having these both is a blessing."
Author Unknown

"Friends are angels who lift us up when our own
wings have trouble remembering how to fly."
Author Unknown

Photo courtesy of Tobin Rogers.

tobinrogers.com

"Family isn't always blood. It's the people in your life who want you in theirs, the ones who accept you for who you are. The ones who would do anything to see you smile & who Love You no matter what."
 Author Unknown

"As night closes in and slumber lulls us to dreamland, let us be thankful for our lives and the friends we share it with."
Anna J. Campbell

"Goodbyes are not forever,
Goodbyes are not the end.
They simply mean
I'll miss you
Until we meet again."
Author Unknown

"True friendship multiplies the good in life and divides its evils. Strive to have friends, for life without friends is like life on a desert island... to find one real friend in a lifetime is good fortune; to keep him is a blessing." Spanish Jesuit and baroque prose writer and philosopher
Baltasar Gracian y Morales (1601 – 1658)

Anna J. Campbell

Photo Courtesy of Paula Hayes .

Chapter 8

Birthday Wishes

For me, this is the best section! I get to use these quotes every year – because everyone has a birthday!

I love that we have an excuse every year to send words of encouragement, humor, and congratulations to those we hold, dear!

Use this opportunity to spread some sunshine and cheer.

~ Anna

Photo courtesy of Kelly Jean.

kellyjphotography.co.uk

"Wishing you a beautiful day with good health and happiness forever! Happy Birthday!"
Author Unknown

Happy Birthday! I hope this year brings you wonderful friends, fun adventures, and happy memories!"
Anna J. Campbell

"If roses grow in Heaven Lord please pick a bunch for me.
Place them in my Mother's arms and tell her they are from me.
Tell her I love her and miss her, and when she turns to smile, place a kiss upon her cheek, and hold her for awhile.
Because remembering her is easy, I do it every day.
But there is an ache within my heart that will never go away."
Author Unknown

"I may not be by your side... Celebrating your special day with you... But I want you to know that I'm thinking of you... and wishing you a wonderful Birthday!"
Author Unknown

"May happiness and sunshine fill your day not only on your birthday, but the whole year through."
Author Unknown

Photo courtesy of Terrance Raper.

terranceraper.myportfolio.com

"Happy Birthday Daughter
We may not say it often
But today is the perfect day to let you know
What a precious gift
You are to us."
Author Unknown

"The warmth and kindness of your heart... Makes
you more beautiful year after year! Wishing you
a very Happy Birthday!"
Author Unknown

"Thinking of you on your birthday and wishing
you happiness always! Happy Birthday!"
Author Unknown

"Hope your special day brings you all that your
heart desires! Here's wishing you a day full of
pleasant surprises! Happy Birthday!"
Author Unknown

"A true gentleman
Sophisticated and wise
Full of warmth and care
And invaluable advice
Full of myriad experiences
A man who I respect
How lucky I am to have
A (father, son, father-in-law) so perfect...
Happy Birthday"
Author Unknown

Photo courtesy of Morgan Lane.

"Happy Birthday Mom
Wishing you a day
As sunny as your smile,
As warm as your heart –
A day as wonderful
As you are."
Author Unknown

"Happy Birthday Mom.
You've helped me enrich my life with your love,
care, guidance and support!
You are not just my Mother,
But my best friend too!
Thank you for always being there for me.
I love you!"
Author Unknown

Photo courtesy of sincerelymedia.com

Chapter 9

Holiday Cheer

It is time for twinkling lights, warm sweaters, and wrapped up surprises! Sometimes, the best surprise of all is a note sent with a simple message from your heart to theirs.

Here are some fun quotes and sayings that carry your message of good tidings and cheer during this holiday season. May your wishes come true!

~ Anna

Photo courtesy of Les Anderson.

"Wish you and your family a joyful, bright, healthy, prosperous and happiest new year ahead! Happy New Year!"
Author Unknown

"A little smile, a word of cheer, a bit of love from someone near, a little gift from one held dear, best wishes for the coming year ~ these make a Merry Christmas!"
Author Unknown

"I'm sending you warm bear hugs, loving kisses and earnest wishes for the wonderful occasion of Christmas. May you have a splendid Christmas filled with lights, songs, and cheer. Merry Christmas and A Happy New Year to you."
Author Unknown

"Happy Thanksgiving. May you have a wonderful holiday with family and friends."
Anna J. Campbell

"May your home be filled with Christmas spirit and the joy of twinkling yellow lights. May you and all you hold dear be surrounded by love this holiday season."
Anna J. Campbell

"There's snowbody I'd rather spend the holidays with than you!"
Author Unknown

"Life is so delicious when you have sweet friends to share it with. Merry Christmas."
Anna J. Campbell

"As we look back over the year, we remember how blessed we are to have you in our lives. We wish you a very Merry Christmas and a very Happy New Year!"
Anna J. Campbell

"Rekindling the joy of Christmas with every snowflake and tinkling bell, we hang upon our tree. We are truly thankful to include you in our family. May you have a beautiful Christmas and a very happy New Year."
Anna J. Campbell

"I love it when every day feels like Christmas! Spending time with loved ones and having good cheer!"
Anna J. Campbell

"Wishing you a beautiful holiday season filled with hope, love, and happiness!"
Anna J. Campbell

Photo courtesy of Egor Myznik

Chapter 10

Seasonal Quotes

"Autumn to winter, winter into spring,
Spring into summer, summer into fall, -
So rolls the changing year, and so we change;
Motion so swift, we know not that we move."
English novelist and poet
Dinah Maria Craik (born Dinah Maria Mulock
1826 - 1887)

Photo courtesy of Ales Krivec.

dreamypixel.com

Spring

"Life stands before me like an eternal spring with new and brilliant clothes."
German mathematician
Carl Friedrich Gauss (born as Johann Carl Friedrich Gauss 1777 – 1855)

"The real voyage of discovery comes not in seeking new landscapes, but in having new eyes."
French novelist, critic, and essayist
Marcel Proust (born as Valentin Louis Georges Eugene Marcel Proust 1871 – 1922)

"It is spring again. The earth is like a child that knows poems by heart."
Bohemian-Austrian poet and novelist
Rainer Maria Rilke (born as Rene Karl Wilhelm Johann Josef Maria Rilke 1875 – 1926)

"The spring came suddenly, bursting upon the world as a child bursts into a room, with a laugh and a shout and hands full of flowers."
Author Unknown

"A kind word is like a Spring day."
Russian Proverb

"And spring arose on the garden fair,
Like the Spirit of Love felt everywhere;
And each flower and herb on Earth's dark breast
Rose from the dreams of its wintry rest."
English romantic poet
Percy Bysshe Shelley (1792 – 1822)

"And after April
When May follows
And the white-throat builds
And all the swallows."
Richard Brinsley Sheridan (R.B. 1751- 1816)

"Spring cleaning doesn't have to be a dreaded list
of chores. It can be a rewarding experience that
helps provide some structure and organization
in your life." Irish theologian and controversialist
Peter Walsh (born Peter Valesius Walsh 1618 –
1688)

"Among the many buds proclaiming May
Decking the fields in holiday array,
Striving who shall surpass in braverie,
Marke the faire flowering of the hawthorne tree
Who finely clothed in a robe of white,
Fills full the wanton eye with May's delight."
Chaucer (1343 – 1400)

"Hedgerows all alive,
With birds and gnats and large white butterflies
Which look as if the Mayflower had caught life
And palpitated forth upon the wind."
E.B. Browning (1806 - 1861)

Photo courtesy of Studio Dekorasyon.

studiodekor.com.tr

"Behold, my friends, the spring is come; the earth has gladly received the embraces of the sun, and we shall soon see the results of their love!"
Hunkpapa Lakota holy man and tribal chief
Sitting Bull (born as Thathanka Iyotake 1831 – 1890)

"The beautiful spring came; and when Nature resumes her loveliness, the human soul is apt to revive also."
African-American writer, nurse and abolitionist speaker
Harriet Ann Jacobs
(also used pseudonym Linda Brent 1813 – 1897)

"Good books are to the young mind what the warming sun and the refreshing rain of spring are to the seeds which have lain dormant in the frosts of winter. They are more, for they may save from that which is worse than death, as well as bless with that which is better than life."
American politician and educational reformer
Horace Mann (1796 – 1859)

"And hark! How blithe the Throstle sings,
He too, is no mean preacher;
Come forth into the light of things
Let Nature be your teacher."
William Wordsworth (1770 – 1850)

Photo courtesy of Nikolay Tchaouchev.

Summer

"The tans will fade but the memories will last forever."
Author Unknown

"The cure for anything is salt water – sweat, tears or the sea."
Danish author used pen names including:
Isak Dinesen, Tania Blixen, Osceola, and Pierre Andrezel. (her name at birth Karen Christenze Dinesen)
(She was also known as Baroness Karen von Blixen-Finecke 1885 – 1962)

"In every girls life, there's a boy she'll never forget and a summer where it all began."
Author Unknown

"I'm toes in the sand kinda girl."
Author Unknown

"There is nothing more beautiful than the way the ocean refuses to stop kissing the shore line, no matter how many times it is sent away."
Author Unknown

"A life without love is like a year without summer."
Swedish Proverb

"At the beach. Time you enjoyed wasting, is not time wasted."
Poet, dramatist, literary critic, and editor
T. S. Elliot (name at birth Thomas Stearns Eliot 1888 – 1965)

"So here's to all those summer nights when my feet hit the sand and the waves break my fall and all my friends around me out number the stars..."
Author Unknown

"At the beach, life is different. Time doesn't move hour to hour but mood to moment. We live by the currents, plan by the tides, and follow the sun."
Author Unknown

"I'm just a summer girl. I wear my flip flops and when I let my hair down that's when the party starts. Who needs a boyfriend? I've got my girlfriends!"
Author Unknown

"Summer is where the girls go barefoot and their hearts are just as free as their toes."
Author Unknown

Photo courtesy of Heather Ford.

themodernlifemrs.com

"The evening comes, the fields are still,
The tinkle of the thirsty rill
Unheard all day ascends again;
Deserted is the half-mown plain,
Silent the swathes! The ringing wain,
The mower's cry, the dogs alarms,
All housed within the sleeping farms!
The business of the day is done,
The last-left hay-maker is gone.
And from the thyme upon the height,
And from the elder-blossom white
And pale dog-roses in the hedge,
And from the mint plant in the sedge,
In puffs of balm the night-air blows
The perfume which the day fore-goes.
And on the pure horizon far,
See, pulsing with the first-born star,
The liquid sky above the hill!
The evening comes, the fields are still."
Matthew Arnold (1822 – 1888)

Photo courtesy of David Ballew.

Autumn

"Autumn, the year's last, loveliest smile."
American romantic poet, journalist, and editor
William Cullen Bryant (1794 – 1878)

"Come little leaves said the wind one day,
Come to the meadows with me and play.
Put on your dresses of red and gold:
For summer is past, and the days grow cold."
American poet
George Cooper (1840 – 1927)

"While ripening corn grew thick and deep,
And here and there men stood to reap,
One morn I put my heart to sleep.
And to the meadows took my way.

The goldfinch on a thistle-head,
Stood scattering seedlets as she fed,
The wrens their pretty gossip spread,
Or joined a random roundelay."
Jean Ingelow (1820 - 1897)

"I'm so glad I live in a world where there are
Octobers."
Canadian author
L.M. Montgomery (Also known as Lucy Maud
Montgomery 1874 – 1942)

Photo courtesy of Kiy Turk.

purposefullyjoyful.com

"Now Autumn's fire burns slowly along the
woods,
And day by day the dead leaves fall and melt,
And night by night the monitory blast
Wails in the key-hole, telling how it pass'd
O'er empty fields, or upland solitudes,
Or grim, wide wave, and now the power is felt
Of melancholy, tenderer in it's moods,
Than any joy indulgent summer dealt."
William Allingham (1824- 1889)

"The leaves fall, the wind blows, and the farm
country slowly changes from the summer
cottons into its winter wools."
American writer and naturalist
Henry Beston (1888 – 1968)

Photo courtesy of Chad Peltola.

Winter

"The beauty of winter is that it makes you appreciate spring." Canadian author **L.M. Montgomery** (Also known as Lucy Maud Montgomery 1874 - 1942)

 "Winter is the time for comfort, for good food and warmth, for the touch of a friendly hand and for a talk beside the fire: it is the time for home." British poet and critic **Dame Edith Louisa Sitwell** (1887 – 1964)

"Sing on sweet thrush, upon the leafless bough,
Sing on sweet bird, I listen to thy strain,
And ages Winter, mid his early reign,
At thy blythe carol, clears his furrowed brow."
Robert Burns (1759 – 1796)

"We are like a snowflake all different in our own beautiful way."
Author Unknown

"The wood are lovely,
dark and deep,
But I have promises to keep,
And miles to go before I sleep,
And miles to go before I sleep."
American poet
Robert Frost (1874 – 1963)

Photo courtesy of Ian Keefe.

iankeefe.ca

Anna J. Campbell

About the Author

Anna J. Campbell is an advocate for regenerative land management, regenerative agriculture and building diverse inclusive communities.

As an active community member, she volunteers with the Willowdale Urban Farm, Cape Fear Food Council (crop mobs), Northside Food Co-op, Cape Fear Sierra Club, and the Global Community Project.

Join me on my next journey of creating a Global Community Map of organizations, groups, and businesses focused on issues impacting the well-being of life on our planet so we can build alliances with each other by sharing skills and resources to accomplish short-term and long-term goals.

These issues include environmental protection, plastic pollution, anti-racism, homelessness, and regenerative agriculture.

GlobalCommunityProject.org

Social Media:

Twitter: @AnnaCampbellMBA
Instagram: Instagram.com/ AnnaCampbellMBA
Facebook: facebook.com/ AnnaCampbellMBA
LinkedIn: linkedin.com/in/annajcampbell/

Websites:
Global network for local leaders creating solutions for issues impacting life on our planet.
GlobalCommunityProject.org

Creating a legacy worth living.
AnnaCampbellMBA.com

Other books written by Anna J. Campbell:
12 Healthy Habits of Business Leadership (2015)
My Monthly Business Journal (2008)

www.ingramcontent.com/pod-product-compliance
Lightning Source LLC
Chambersburg PA
CBHW070359290526
45790CB00004B/1552